To my mother, for giving me the richest human gift— unconditional love. And to my father, for showing me the gift of ongoing learning.

CONTENTS

Acknowledgments   vi

PART I   VISIONS OF EXCELLENCE

Chapter 1   The Wheel of Excellence   3

Chapter 2   A Journey to Excellence   21

PART II   COMMITTING TO EXCELLENCE

Chapter 3   Commitment to Excellence   39

Chapter 4   Focused Connection to Goals   47

Chapter 5   Meaningful Goals   59

Chapter 6   Positive Perspectives   69

**PART III   MENTAL PREPARATION
FOR EXCELLENCE**

Chapter 7   Mission to Excellence   79

Chapter 8   Quest for Consistency   91

Chapter 9   Positive Images   107

Chapter 10   Relaxation and Intensity   121

Chapter 11   Distraction Control   133